APPLE'S HOMEKIT SMART HOME
AUTOMATION SYSTEM HANDBOOK

Discover How to Build Your Own
Smart Home Using Apple's New HomeKit App

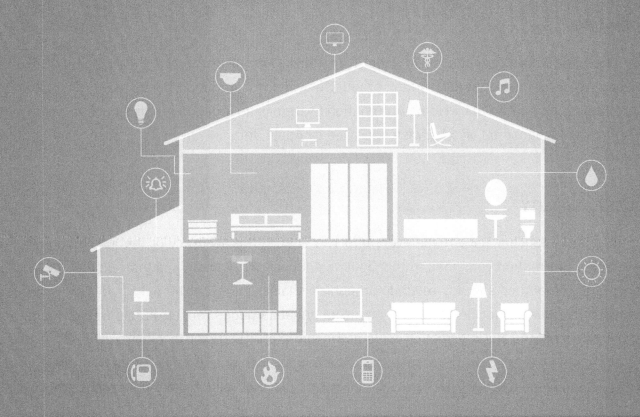

GERARD O'DRISCOLL

COPYRIGHT NOTICE & DISCLAIMER NOTICE

(Please Read This Before Using This Book)

DEFINITIVE GUIDE TO APPLE'S HOMEKIT SMART HOME AUTOMATION SYSTEM

Copyright ©2016 HomeMentors

NOTICE OF RIGHTS

All rights reserved. No part of this book may be reproduced or transmitted in any manner whatsoever without written permission except in the case of brief quotations embodied in critical articles or reviews. Purchase of the electronic version of this document grants the purchaser permission to create copies for personal use. The document cannot be resold or distributed. No part of the electronic version of this document may be reproduced in any manner whatsoever without written permission.

TRADEMARKS

HomeKit is a trademark of Apple, Inc. All other trademarks are the property of their respective owners. HomeMentors is not associated with any product or vendor mentioned in this book. The Definitive Guide to Apple's HomeKit Smart Home Automation System is an independent publication and has not been authorized, sponsored or otherwise approved by Apple, Inc.

NOTICE OF LIABILITY

The author and publisher have made every effort to ensure the accuracy of the information herein. However, the information contained in this book is sold without warranty, either express or implied. Furthermore, the author and any related companies shall in no event be held liable for any direct, indirect, punitive, special, incidental or other consequential damages caused either directly or indirectly by instructions, content, and information contained in this book. If you wish to follow guidelines contained in this book, then you are taking full responsibility for your own actions. The content in this book are merely guidelines and there are no hard and fast rules on using Apple HomeKit Smart Home devices.

CONTENTS

COPYRIGHT NOTICE & DISCLAIMER NOTICE II

THE BOOKS COMPANION VIDEO COURSE 3

OTHER BOOKS IN THE ESSENTIAL GUIDE TO SMART HOME AUTOMATION SERIES 3

    Before We Begin and Free Gifts 4

WHO SHOULD READ THIS BOOK? 5

HOW TO USE THIS BOOK? 5

INTRODUCTION TO APPLE HOMEKIT 7

KEY HOMEKIT BENEFITS TO HOMEOWNERS 7

APPLE HOMEKIT TIMELINE 11

    How Apple Homekit Works 11

THE HOME APP 13

CONTROL CENTER MANAGEMENT OF YOUR SMART HOME DEVICES 16

THIRD PARTY HOMEKIT APPS 17

HOW TO INITIALLY SETUP HOMEKIT ON YOUR IPHONE, IPAD OR IPOD 18

INSTALLING YOUR HOMEKIT ENABLED SMART HOME 21

    Homekit Door & Window Sensors 21

    Homekit Smart Plugs 25

    Homekit Smart Lighting Bulbs 25

HOMEKIT SMART THERMOSTATS 27

    Setting up a HomeKit Thermostat 27

HOMEKIT IP CAMERAS 28

    Configuring your IP camera to connect with Apple HomeKit 28

HOMEKIT DOORBELLS 29

HOMEKIT SMART LOCKS 30

NON-HOMEKIT COMPLIANT SMART HOME PRODUCTS 31

ORGANIZING YOUR SMART HOME DEVICES USING HOMEKIT 32

USING SIRI TO CONTROL YOUR HOMEKIT DEVICES 33

USING HOMEKIT ON YOUR WRIST 34

    Popular uses of Apple Watch Homekit Apps 35

    Controlling your Apple Home over the Internet 36

    Setting Up your Apple Tv 4 as a Home Hub 36

    Setting Up your Ipad as a Home Hub 37

    Using Homekit to Automate Your Home 38

HELPING FAMILY MEMBERS INTERACT WITH YOUR SMART HOME 39

SOLVING HOMEKIT ISSUES 40

FINAL THOUGHTS 42

ABOUT THE **AUTHOR** **44**

DEDICATION 45

THE BOOKS COMPANION VIDEO COURSE 46

WOULD YOU LIKE TO HEAR MORE ABOUT SMART HOMES & RECEIVE A FREE EBOOK? 47

OTHER BOOKS IN THE ESSENTIAL GUIDE TO SMART HOME AUTOMATION SERIES 48

A FAVOR! 48

A REMINDER ABOUT UPDATES 48

THE BOOKS COMPANION VIDEO COURSE

To help guide you through building your own Apple Smart Home, I recently produced a companion video training course titled: *How to Build Your Own Smart Home Automation System Using Apple HomeKit Products*.

The regular price of the course is $97, however, for a limited time, you can enroll in the course for $47!

Click Here to get $50 discount off the regular price today before the limited number of coupons run out!

OTHER BOOKS IN THE ESSENTIAL GUIDE TO SMART HOME AUTOMATION SERIES

Essential Guide to Smart Home Automation Safety & Security

Essential Guide to Smart Bulbs & Lighting Control

Essential Guide to Smart Home Entertainment

Essential Guide to Smart Homes For Aging Adults

Essential Guide to Nest Smart Home Automation System

Essential Guide to Samsung SmartThings Smart Home Automation System

Essential Guide to Apple's HomeKit Smart Home Automation System

Smart Home Automation Essential Guides Box Set

Please also note that most of our books are now available in paperback, so if you still prefer to read a print version of a book, you can find them on Amazon.

BEFORE WE BEGIN AND FREE GIFTS

Before we start, I just want to remind you about the free updates for this book. The Apple HomeKit system is still in its infancy and has its limitations, which are expected to be mitigated over time. The list of products compatible with the framework continues to evolve. Staying on top of this is my job! Therefore, could I suggest that you **Sign Up for Our Email List** and keep yourself abreast of updates as they happen.

| Click Here to Download Your Free Copy of the '8 Week Blueprint on Building a Smart Home'. A summarized action plan, which you can follow over the coming weeks, months and indeed years.

Check Out the Plan Here. | *[Image of HomeMentors.com blueprint table showing action plan items 1.0–2.1 with tick boxes]* |

WHO SHOULD READ THIS BOOK?

This book is intended to be read by the following people:

- Homeowners interested in controlling their lighting, alarm, safety, heating and entertainment systems on their iPhones, iPads or Apple Watches while out and about or at home.

- Homebuilders interested in identifying Apple-based smart home automation ideas that will differentiate their offerings and improve overall property sales.

- Anyone else curious about how to setup an Apple HomeKit based smart home system at a reasonable cost!

HOW TO USE THIS BOOK?

Feel free to dip in and out of different sections, but we suggest reading the full book from beginning to end to get a good sense of the Apple HomeKit smart home system. The book aims to answer several questions that you may have about Apple's smart home system such as:

- What is the Apple HomeKit smart home system?
- How does HomeKit operate and work?
- What are the key benefits of HomeKit?
- How to setup and configure your HomeKit based smart Home?
- How to introduce and organize HomeKit in your home?
- How to control and manage HomeKit smart Home products?
- Plus, lots more!

INTRODUCTION TO APPLE HOMEKIT

HomeKit is Apple's initiative to bring smart home automation to nearly a billion mobile devices. It was unveiled alongside iOS 8 in the middle of 2014.

Apple, yes Apple, has set its sights on bringing smart home automation products and services to the masses. Rather than releasing its own line of products, Apple announced a new ecosystem in 2014 called HomeKit. The name itself uses a combination of "Home" from the popular term home automation and applies 'Kit' to the end of the name to represent the availability of a "kit" for software developers.

Insight from Gerard:

HomeKit availability is limited to the Apple ecosystem of products, namely iPads, Apple computers, iPhones and Apple Watches.

HomeKit acts as the glue that holds smart homes together, invisibly working to allow each smart thermostat, door camera, security sensor, leak detector, or IP camera to talk to the others with Apple verbal instructions.

The main purpose of HomeKit is to simplify the management and control of a home that has various smart devices installed from multiple vendors.

KEY HOMEKIT BENEFITS TO HOMEOWNERS

As with everything in life, the benefits of motivating yourself and spending money needs to produce some tangible results! Although the benefits of adding automation to your home will vary from person to person, there are some general benefits that most people can enjoy as result of adding Apple HomeKit products to their property:

- **HomeKit is Simple to Use** – Once installed, an Apple-based smart home system provides easy control of all your lights, heating, security and entertainment systems via a tablet, smartphone or Apple computer.

- **Simplification of the Smart Home Industry** – The smart home ecosystem includes a myriad of incompatible products and communication protocols. Apple HomeKit simplifies this environment.

- **HomeKit is Expandable** – HomeKit lets you build your Smart Home as your needs grow – one solution at a time. As an example, some people start with a basic energy management kit comprising of smart bulbs and plugs. Once people get comfortable with this setup, they often start to build out their HomeKit network through the addition of various other types of smart devices. In the past, integrated smart home systems were typically installed by specialists, which often proved to be quite expensive. With HomeKit, you will be able to organically expand your system in a step-by-step manner.

- **HomeKit is Secure –** Security is paramount when it comes to your home and is a major concern for most of us. Obvious concerns include what happens if someone steals my phone or will I be able to open the front door lock if for whatever reason, I forget my password. Apple addresses these concerns by including five key security mechanisms that guarantee against unauthorized third parties interfering with your in-home network:

① Apple HomeKit does not allow bridged devices to trigger smart home products such as smart locks that provide physical access to your home.

② HomeKit includes end-to-end encryption and authentication between a smartphone, Apple watch, iPod or iPad and the various HomeKit certified smart home devices – meaning nobody but you and your family can get access.

③ As pictured below, a setup code, typically displayed on the packaging is required during the initial configuration.

④ Apple HomeKit also features sophisticated privacy layers to minimize threats from external hackers. For instance, details about your home are not stored on Apple servers.

⑤ HomeKit mandates that Apps can only be used in the foreground. In other words, it will be immediately obvious to you by looking at your iPhone if a third party hacker attempts to mess around with your connected home products.

⑥ Although HomeKit allows you to control certain devices when your iOS device is locked; it does prohibit control of products such as smart locks unless your iOS device has been unlocked.

- **Improved Comfort & Convenience** – Apple HomeKit systems allow you to set up "scenes" that will increase comfort levels at home. Scenes are normally used to perform a number of actions at a particular instance in time. For instance, I have an "ALL LIGHTS OFF" scene on my iPhone that switches all lights OFF around the house – it's handier than jumping out of a warm bed on a cold Irish winter's night and turning off the light in the bathroom.

- **Supports Voice Control** – HomeKit integrates well with Siri virtual voice assistant, Apple's virtual personal assistant allows you to use simple voice commands to control individual in-home smart devices and groups of devices.

Although the use of voice activation technologies such as Siri has experienced limited traction; the Siri technology is a prominent feature of HomeKit enabled smart homes. The feature works quite well at home because your iPhone or iPad is connected to your home network. However, Siri commands will

Insight from Gerard:

Using Siri to interface with your home is as simple as pressing the home button on your iOS device and speaking the desired commands. This level of user friendliness is enabled because Siri is an integral part of the operating system.

Apple's Homekit Smart Home

not operate outside of your home unless you install an Apple TV - requires a fourth generation Apple TV.

So for instance; issuing a "Goodnight Siri" command at home would initiate a number of actions such as locking all doors, turning lights off, closing the garage door and turning off TVs.

However, if you were to issue the exact same voice command, while away from home; and you did not have an Apple TV installed, then nothing would happen.

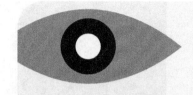

Insight from Gerard:

HomeKit software support was added to Apple TV at the end of 2014.

- **Easy Setup –** Apple's HomeKit guides you through the process of configuring various types of home automation devices, ranging from smart bulbs and thermostats to water leak detectors and networked cameras. The process of adding a new smart home product to your Apple-based smart home is quick and easy.

- **Supports a Single App –** One of the key criticisms of smart homes at the moment is the absence of a singular and robust App that can be used to control your home from a single point. At present, this functionality is typically regulated to high-end systems. For people who want to cost effectively add smart features to their homes they will typically need to use multiple apps to control their home; one for your smart lock, one for your lights, one for your smart thermostat and so on. Apple's Home allows you do all of this under one singular App.

- **Remote Access –** Similar to other smart home systems, Apple HomeKit provides the ability to use your iPhone, Apple Watch, or iPad to control your home over the Internet. Let's say you are away for the weekend, and you are unsure as to whether or not you locked the back door when leaving. To improve peace of mind, HomeKit allows you open up a smartphone app and verify that the smart lock installed in the back door is set to LOCKED.

- **No Need to Purchase a Separate Hub –** With HomeKit, your Apple TV or iPad acts as the controller for your entire range of smart home connected devices. This negates the need to purchase a hub, which not only adds additional costs but becomes yet another hardware device to setup and maintain.

- **Build your Apple Smart Home Piece by Piece –** The beauty about Apple HomeKit is that it allows you to grow your smart home one system at a time. So rather than initially going out and purchasing an expensive home automation system, HomeKit allows you to purchase individual devices that solve a particular problem in your home.

APPLE HOMEKIT TIMELINE

Apple's HomeKit is a key part of the smart home marketplace. Here are some key milestones over the past two years:

- Apple started slowly at first by debuting HomeKit back in 2014. In June of that year, it announced partnerships with various manufacturers.
- First HomeKit-enabled products were released in June 2015.
- Apple's Home app is launched in 2016 as part of iOS 10 and gets prime real estate on millions of iOS device screens around the world.

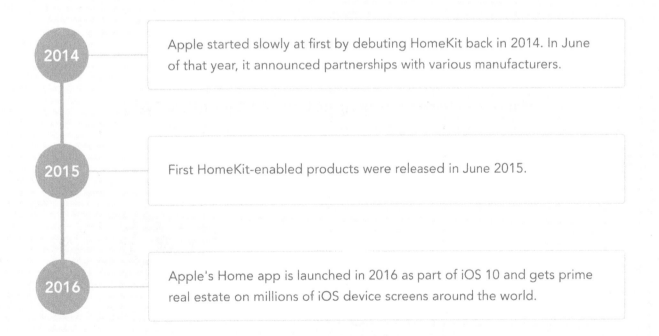

Figure 1 –Apple HomeKit Timeline

HOW APPLE HOMEKIT WORKS

A highly simplified graphical view of how the different elements of a typical Apple HomeKit system fit together are provided below:

ELEMENTS OF AN APPLE HOMEKIT END-TO-END SYSTEM

Figure 2 – Elements of an Apple HomeKit End-to-End System

THE FEATURES OF THE DIAGRAM ABOVE ARE:

① **An iOS Device –** HomeKit only works with Apple products, namely: computers, iPhones, watches and iPads.

② **An App -** Most manufacturers have released device-specific apps; however, Apple have recently launched their own App aptly titled 'Home' that acts as a centralized mechanism for managing all your HomeKit compatible connected devices. The Home App is recognizable as an icon of a house on your iOS device.

③ **Apple iCloud Servers –** iCloud is an integral part of the Apple HomeKit framework and provides various levels of functionality, including:

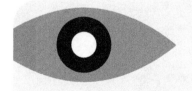

Insight from Gerard:

In the literature used by Apple to describe their smart home ecosystem, the company often uses the term 'accessory' to describe a smart home product or device.

Apple's Homekit Smart Home

- Secure remote access, providing connectivity with your smart-home devices from anywhere in the world

- Sending notifications to you or a family member when away from home.

- Synchronizing smart home configuration information that resides on your primary iOS device with other iOS devices in the household.

④ **HomeKit Enabled Smart Home Products –** Smart home products come in different form factors ranging from smart locks and garage door openers to smart bulbs, sensors, smart plugs, and thermostats. To use HomeKit make sure that whatever product you are installing that if includes the 'Works with Apple Homekit' logo on its packaging. This logo confirms that the product has been fully approved and certified by Apple.

⑤ **A Home Wi-Fi Network –** It is really important that you build a robust and reliable Wi-Fi network capable of supporting your Apple Smart Home. HomeKit uses Wi-Fi for communication between iOS devices and the various smart products installed around your house.

⑥ **An Apple TV or iPad (Optional) –** The Apple TV is installed if you want to avail of Siri functionality and remotely connect to your smart devices when away from home. So once a voice or app command is issued, your iOS device sends the command onwards to the Apple TV, which in turn passes it to the relevant smart home device. It should also be borne in mind that an iPad permanently left at home can also provide similar functionality.

Insight from Gerard:

This functionality will only work correctly with version 10 and above of the software and when your Apple TV hardware is a third generation or above.

THE HOME APP

HomeKit enabled smart home products designed for specific functions in your home come with their own dedicated apps.

Want to turn off the heat, dim the lights, unlock your door and view your cameras? No problem, but you'll need four separate apps! Over time, multiple apps proliferate on your phone once you start to increase the number of smart products installed in your home.

Apple has solved this problem in recent times by releasing a unified app for HomeKit compatible connected devices titled 'Home'.

The Home app is embedded into the iOS 10 and watchOS3 operating systems.

The Home app acts as a control center and lets you turn on lights, unlock doors, and even raise your window shades — all at once if you like.

HERE ARE SOME KEY BENEFITS OF HOME:

- It makes it easier to manage your smart home in one spot, without needing to open up a specific app for each individual smart home device.

- The Home app interface is clean, has a modern look, simple to use and supports the recognizable 'wibbly wobbly' icon drag-and-drop functionality familiar to all iOS users.

- You can access Home on the main screen or within the control center.

- Home is a unified app that acts as a centralized hub to manage all your HomeKit compatible connected devices. No more need for need for countless proprietary apps.

- Home fully supports 3D Touch functionality (new technology senses how deeply users press the display). This capability allows you to quickly adjust temperature, color, and brightness levels.

- Home also lets you personalize the app experience through changeable wallpapers that are applied in the background. For instance, you can apply a unique wallpaper to each room.

- Notes is an unusual yet innovative feature that allows family members to input little messages that can be viewed by anyone who has access to the Home app. This capability is popular amongst landlords who own HomeKit controlled properties and want to leave notes for their tenants.

- Notifications and alerts to your iPhone, iPad, or Apple Watch are supported for certain HomeKit-enabled smart home products.

When Home is running on your iOS device, you will see a menu bar that runs along the bottom of the app containing three tabs: Home, Rooms, and Automation:

Home – When you initially launch the App, you'll see your home's name big and bold near the top of the screen. A general summary overview is provided of what's going on in your house just below your home's name. This overview provides the statuses of your various HomeKit enabled smart home devices. For instance, this status message might provide the current temperature level and how many lights are turned on around the house.

This initial screen also offers you a collage of favorite scenes and connected home devices in the one place, allowing you to quickly control smart devices used on a frequent basis.

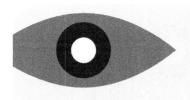

Insight from Gerard:

Long pressing a button can provide more detailed settings for some connected household devices. For instance, brightness and color controls appear for Philips Hue bulbs.

In addition to providing control of the various smart home, devices installed around your home you can also run 'scenes' inside here. For those of you who have not previously encountered the term 'scene' – A scene consists of a collection of smart home settings that can get activated all at once. For instance; you may have a scene on your Apple device called 'I'm Leaving' that turns off all the lights in the house and switches your smart thermostats to off mode.

Another cool thing you can do in the screen is change between multiple properties Very helpful for landlords who own multiple rental properties equipped with HomeKit enabled products. Not only can you switch between houses but the home screen allows you to easily rearrange your favorite devices and scenes. Simply tap the 'edit' button and the icons go all **wibbly wobbly** like you commonly see on an iOS device. When in this mode you are able to move and reorder both scene and smart home device icons around your screen. In other words, it allows you to personalize the experience.

Up in the corner of the screen, you will see a '+' icon that allows you to add an accessory (aka a smart home product) or a new customized scene. The addition of scenes and new devices within the app is an easy and intuitive process.

So that pretty much covers the Home screen within the Apple Home App. Next, let's pop over to the Rooms tab.

Rooms – HomeKit allows you to manage your smart home devices on a more granular basis by sorting your smart devices by location. It is considered best practice to organize your smart home devices according to which room they're physically in.

To create a room; simply run through the following actions:

- Open the Home app and tap the Rooms tab at the bottom.
- Tap the ≡ icon on the upper left corner of the screen.
- Next up, tap Add Room on the top left-hand corner of the screen.
- On this next screen; you will be able to name your room and add a background image.

If we go back to the Rooms page; you will notice the + icon on the top right-hand portion of the screen. This allows you to add a scene or a smart home product to each of the rooms. This portion of the Home app also allows you to drill into each of these rooms allowing you to view individually home devices installed in each of the particular rooms.

If you want to view your smart home products on a room-by-room basis, then you can simply swipe to the left to scroll through your various rooms.

Insight from Gerard:

You can also navigate between rooms by swiping left and right across the screen.

Automation – Lastly, let's take a more in-depth look at the Automation tab of the Home App. As the name infers this area of the Home App is full of ways that you can automate your home. Here you can use various types of rules and timers to help your smart home anticipate your family's daily requirements.

To use the awesome features on this tab, make sure that there is an Apple TV 4 or an iPad with iOS 10 setup as a hub in your home.

Another cool feature of the Home App is the ability to assign particular devices and indeed scenes to a favorites menu. We'll explore the magic of automation further on in the book.

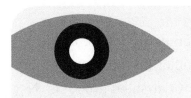

Insight from Gerard:

If you try and use the automation area of the app, you'll see a dialog box in Home telling you to install an Apple TV 4 or an iPad in Home Hub mode.

CONTROL CENTER MANAGEMENT OF YOUR SMART HOME DEVICES

One of the key features of iOS 10 is the ability to easily manage your smart home directly within the control center of your iOS device. The translucent Control Centre gives you quick and direct access to commonly used settings and apps from anywhere in iOS—including the lock screen.

To access your smart home within Control Center, swipe up from the bottom of the screen and swipe left to access your Apple certified smart home products.

Here at the smart home panel, you will see your favorite smart home products. From here you can quickly and elegantly control various types of smart home devices. There are four ways to interact with app icons and tiles, namely:

① *Tapping* – One quick touch that creates an immediate action.

② *Toggling* – Used on a large on-screen button to turn smart home products on or off.

③ *Sliding* – This technique is normally used to adjust temperature and dimming levels

④ *Press and hold* - This interaction invokes a full-screen controller that contains more options for particular categories of smart home products. A smart bulb that supports a range of colors is a good example of where this interaction type might be used.

Insight from Gerard:

In the current iteration of the software nine of your favorite smart home products and eight favorite scenes are supported within the panel of your iPhone. This number grows to 12 connected devices and 12 scenes for larger iOS devices, namely the iPad Pro.

To close Control Center, swipe down, tap the top of the screen, or press the Home button.

It is also worth noting that Home has lock screen integration for viewing alerts and device status without having to unlock an iPhone.

THIRD PARTY HOMEKIT APPS

The Apple Home app is a great solution for quickly accessing and controlling your HomeKit-enabled devices.

However, in addition to using the default Home App, Apple has chosen to allow third parties to provide their own HomeKit interfaces. These third-party apps are typically available free when you purchase a connected device. As the Home App does not provide everything for all of your HomeKit devices, these Apps can provide a more granular mechanism for controlling individual products and facilitating firmware upgrades. Another interesting feature of third-party HomeKit apps is that they also can be used as a unified app, providing control of multiple HomeKit devices. In other words, devices from multiple vendors are visible within the third-party app; giving you greater flexibility in choosing a smart home app that works best for you. Gone are the days of been locked into using an App from a single provider. Pictured below is an example of a popular third party app used to power Elgato HomeKit certified devices.

HOW TO INITIALLY SETUP HOMEKIT ON YOUR IPHONE, IPAD OR IPOD

In the HomeKit system, unique names get applied to your home, rooms and each individual smart home device.

These names are stored in a database on your iOS device; that is accessible via Siri. Furthermore, you will also need to apply names to specific functions.

Here are the initial steps required to add HomeKit functionality to your home:

Insight from Gerard:

Having all of your smart home devices and systems in one place improves the overall experience of interacting with your home and in my mind represents a game changer for the industry as a whole.

Apple's Homekit Smart Home

STEP 1: CONFIGURE IOS DEVICE SETTINGS

To get started with your Apple-based smart home, you first need to make sure that you're logged into your iCloud account and Home is enabled within the iCloud menu. Also from the iCloud menu, you will also need to turn on Keychain as pictured below.

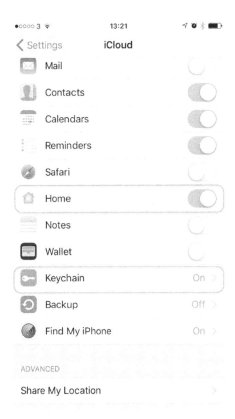

iPhone Settings.PNG

STEP 2: LAUNCH 'HOME' APP

The Home App resides on your main iPhone or iPad screen; and once launched the first time you will be met with the welcome screen followed by a few steps to get started, including naming your home. Most people starting out accept the default name – *My Home*.

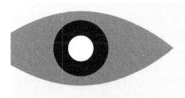

Insight from Gerard:

The app will display HomeKit devices you already have up and running.

Apple's Homekit Smart Home

STEP 3: ADD SMART HOME DEVICES

Start adding various smart home products to the configuration.

STEP 4: ADD ROOM NAMES TO THE APP

Once your home is named; the Home app walks you through the naming of various rooms. At this point, a planning worksheet should be useful in terms of inputting the room data in a structured manner.

The information provided above is included in a profile which gets stored locally and within your personal iCloud account.

INSTALLING YOUR HOMEKIT ENABLED SMART HOME

Using HomeKit to its fullest capabilities requires the installation of an array of sensors and connected devices around your home to measure environmental conditions and detect the presence of people moving about. Each of these HomeKit compliant devices includes some common features, namely:

- An Apple designed HomeKit chip and software that provide secure communications between apps running on iOS devices.
- An app that is typically used for setup.
- HomeKit-enabled accessories have an official "Works with Apple HomeKit" badge on the product packaging.

There are a growing number of smart home products with HomeKit capabilities coming to market, ranging from being able to switch off lamps around the house with a smartphone, to automatically executing sophisticated music, heating, security and lighting control tasks. HomeKit certified products are identifiable in shops and online through labels displayed on the packaging of smart home products.

The presence of the logo instills an element of confidence that the product has been certified by Apple to work in your home.

The types of products supported by Apple HomeKit and how to set them up are explained in the following sections.

HOMEKIT DOOR & WINDOW SENSORS

First, we have door and window contact sensors. These sensors can act in a variety of scenarios to increase your security and safety levels.

One of the nice things about HomeKit door and window sensors is that they connect directly to your iPhone or iPad using Bluetooth or Wi-Fi smart networking technology, without requiring a hub, gateway or bridge.

Setting up a HomeKit sensor takes just a few minutes. Here are the steps involved with getting it up and running.

① To start using HomeKit, the latest version of iOS software needs to be running on your iPhone, iPad or iPod.

② Previously you needed to download the app that accompanies your HomeKit door and window sensor. With Home all, you need to do is simply launch the app launch.

③ Once the main screen appears, select the 'Add Accessory' option.

④ The Select an accessory to add to Home page appears and has identified the 'Eve Door'.

Apple's Homekit Smart Home

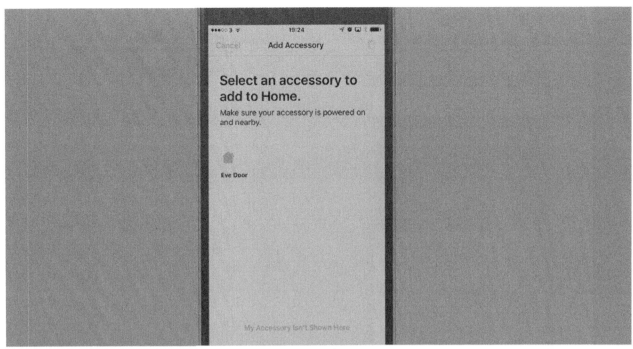

⑤ Similar to Bluetooth; you will need to enter a short pairing code when adding each smart home device to your smartphone app. In the Home app, you will next be prompted for the HomeKit Setup Code; a code that is applied to your smart home device in the form of a sticker. The Home App will use your iPhone's or iPads camera to enter this code.

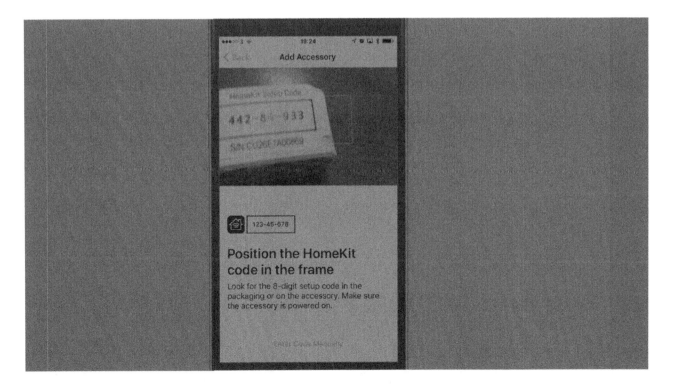

Apple's Homekit Smart Home

⑥ Pairing commences as shown below.

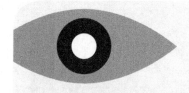

Insight from Gerard:

HomeKit uses Wireless Accessory Configuration (WAC) to simplify the pairing process. In essence, WAC eliminates the need to input the Wi-Fi password for your network, because these details are stored on your iPhone or iPad. Under WAC, these details are transmitted to the HomeKit certified device during the pairing process.

⑦ After a short period of time; your Home App will confirm that the sensor has been successfully included in your HomeKit based Smart Home

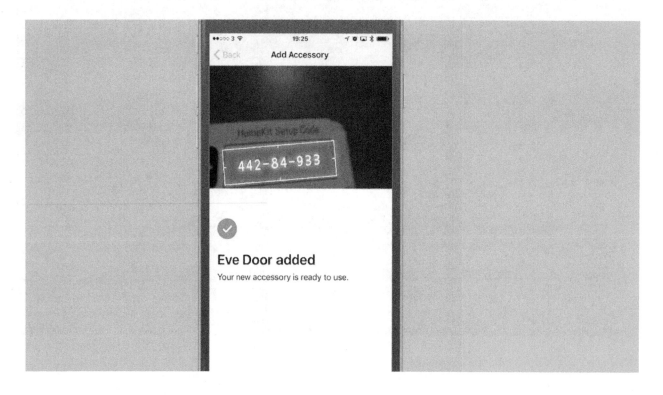

Apple's Homekit Smart Home

Once the sensor is paired; it's simply a matter of installing your new sensor in a suitable location such as a door or window in this case.

As you can see, the setup is straightforward.

HOMEKIT SMART PLUGS

So what is the first HomeKit certified smart product should people buy?

My own opinion is that you should initially buy a connected product that solves some type of easy problem or improves a particular convenience. For instance, you may want a certain light to turn on during particular times of the day.

Smart plugs are a great entry-level product for people; because they are low cost and are easily installed.

HomeKit enabled smart plugs allow you to turn connected pluggable lamp Modules ON and OFF remotely. These modules are also controllable via the Home app, allowing you to ensure optimal efficiency.

Installation is simple; you just plug your kitchen appliance, lamp or whatever into the switch, which in turn gets plugged into the main socket on the wall. Some of the more advanced smart plugs on the market also allow you to see how much energy your devices use in real time.

Let's now move on to another popular category of HomeKit compatible products, smart bulbs.

HOMEKIT SMART LIGHTING BULBS

Once installed, HomeKit smart lights allow any member of your household to use their own iPhone, Apple watch or iPad to control the lights. Furthermore, for convenience and safety purposes, existing conventional wall switches can also be used to turn your smart bulb ON and OFF - useful if your iPhone is not at hand.

In order to link smart bulbs with HomeKit many of the systems currently available require a separate bridge device that is connected directly into your router.

Key Features

Here are a few things you can do with HomeKit enabled smart bulbs which include:

- **Setup Lighting Scenes –** This feature allows you to precisely configure which lights come on at particular intervals and how they come ON and OFF.

- **Use Siri virtual voice assistant to Control your Home Lights –** With this feature, you can speak into your iOS device and tell your lights to do all kinds of cool things ranging from basic ON/OFF functionality to adjusting brightness levels and changing colors.

- **Apply Color Changing –** The vast arrays of colors supported by LEDs built into smart bulbs can be used to design creative lighting shows and effects.

- **Integration with other Smart Home Systems –** HomeKit smart bulbs can be configured to interface with other HomeKit and indeed non-HomeKit compliant smart home products.

Setting Up A HomeKit Smart Lighting System

A typical smart lighting HomeKit installation consists of an iOS app, a bridge device and various smart bulbs located in light fixtures around your home.

The bridge device has its own built-in fingernail sized dedicated wireless HomeKit chip. The integration of a wireless chip ensures compliance with the HomeKit framework.

Setting up a HomeKit lighting system is pretty simple. For instance, here are the steps that I carried out to connect the latest edition of the Philips Hue bridge to the O'Driscoll's in-home network.

① Make sure your light switch is in the off position.

② Unbox, connect the bridge to your router with an Ethernet cable and power up.

③ Download the free app.

④ Open the app and tap the button on your bridge to pair the two smart home devices.

⑤ Next, use your iPhone camera to take a picture of the HomeKit code sticker when prompted.

⑥ Within seconds of scanning the code, the bridge will securely pair to your iPhone.

⑦ Create a cloud account.

⑧ Screw the bulbs into your existing light fittings - needed for rewiring at your light switches.

Apple's Homekit Smart Home

⑨ Turn on your wall light switches.

⑩ Once the bridge is running, use the smart bulbs app to name bulbs and create various types of scenes.

Now that you have a feel for what HomeKit is all about; let's now move onto smart home products that require more sophisticated installs.

HOMEKIT SMART THERMOSTATS

An app combined with a HomeKit thermostat allows you to interface with your heating or cooling system on a real-time basis from anywhere in the world. Once configured correctly, smart thermostats allow you to:

- Remotely raise and lower the temperature.
- Set up modes and schedules that match your daily lifestyle.
- Use an app to turn the heating system ON or OFF from any part of the world!

Setting Up A HomeKit Thermostat

The setup of a HomeKit thermostat, typically involves 5 steps, namely:

① Identifying the type of heating and cooling system in your home.

② Removing the existing thermostat.

③ Physically installing and wiring up your HomeKit thermostat.

④ Downloading and launching the mobile app associated with the device.

⑤ Following the step-by-step instructions in the app to configure and personalize your HomeKit thermostat.

HOMEKIT IP CAMERAS

Before we delve into the topic of connecting an IP camera to your HomeKit system, let's take a minute to outline the main features of IP cameras:

- **High-quality video content:** IP cameras are digital and produce a high-resolution video that is more accurate and clear when compared to viewing an analog video stream.

- **Indoor and outdoor support:** Indoor IP cameras keep an eye on a particular room whereas outdoor IP cameras are weatherproof and monitor your garden or driveway.

- **PoE support:** Another cool feature of IP cameras is their support for a networking technology called Power over Ethernet (PoE). This technology integrates power into a standard home networking infrastructure. It enables power to be provided to the network device, such as an IP network camera, using the same cable that is used for the network connection.

- **PTZ support:** PTZ is an abbreviation for Pan, Tilt and Zoom. As the name implies, this feature allows you to cover quite a large area and get a good overview of what is happening in your home.

- **Wi-Fi support:** Let's not forget about Wi-Fi; IP cameras typically provide Wi-Fi connectivity. In the context of an Apple smart home system install, Wi-Fi is the method used to stream images to an iPhone, iPad, or iWatch.

- **Two-way audio:** Some IP camera models come with a built-in microphone allowing you to listen-in to conversations and noises from intruders. In addition to a microphone, some models include an internal speaker or a line out connector that allows you to install some external speakers. Speakers allow you to issue warnings to your intruder in real time whilst he or she is up to no good in your home.

Now that you have zoned in on a particular IP camera make and model, the next step is to physically install and integrate with your Apple smart home system.

Configuring your IP camera to connect with Apple HomeKit

For those who have limited computer or IT skills, getting an IP camera up and running can be daunting for some people. Fortunately, the cycle of getting an IP camera to send back streaming video to an iOS device is relatively straightforward. The key steps required to start using an IP camera with your Apple smart home are as follows:

① Download the app for your IP camera.

② Setup an online account to store videos from your IP camera.

③ Setup and pair using the Home app.

HOMEKIT DOORBELLS

There's no part of the modern home that isn't touched in some way by smart technology. This isn't a quirk of futuristic science destined for a dead end. Smart products are a rapidly maturing line of appliances and devices being manufactured by world-leading companies, and the doorbell is next to be made over, recreated with wireless connectivity and additional functionality. Push the button on your boring, conventional doorbell and you blindly walk your hallway with a frown of puzzlement. The chime has caught your attention, but you have no idea who's at the door. This accepted routine is being entirely rewritten by the latest generation of smart doorbells. Firstly, when the illuminated doorbell is depressed, you're no longer blind to who's out there. A smart doorbell has digital sight, the ability to transmit video of the person outside through a Wi-Fi connection thanks to a built-in camera. This alone is a blessing in our security-conscious age, but you also have the option to talk to the person through an integrated intercom.

While basic approaches to practical smart doorbells act as little more than a high-tech intercom, fully-equipped HomeKit enabled models are high-security concepts granting convenience and safety with WiFi connectivity.

You can check who's at the door from the comfort of your seat, picking up your iOS device to see video of the potential guest and be able to make a decision to allow entry by switching to your Home App. If you don't recognize the face, tap another button and converse with the stranger to learn why they're intruding on your precious quiet time. It may seem like a lazy way to answer the door, but think of the advantages. Instead of lazing on your couch, you might instead be on vacation or stuck at work.

The point is, your voice issues from the little speaker on the smart doorbell, leaving the person at the door with the impression of you inside your home!

HOMEKIT SMART LOCKS

The general sense that I get from neighbors and friends is that people are wary of using smart locks. This is perfectly understandable as we have all been using regular locks and keys for many years.

Smart locks use advanced recognition technology, access codes, combinations of Wi-Fi and Bluetooth, all to simplify and hasten your entry to the sanctuary of your home. Smart locks are always on guard, waiting for an encrypted virtual key to be transmitted from your phone. One of the biggest selling points of smart locks is the ability to control who goes in and out of your home and when. Smart locks are relatively new to the market and up to recently could only be remotely controlled with a mobile app.

The recent addition of HomeKit to smart locks makes these devices more appealing to general consumers. Thanks to HomeKit, you can now speak to your iPhone or Apple Watch and say things like "Open the door" and your door magically unlocks.

How often have we all left home in the morning and a nagging doubt surfaces in the back of our minds sometime during the day about whether or not the door is locked? HomeKit locks allow you to check the status of your door.

Insight from Gerard:

HomeKit locks include a requirement to unlock your screen prior to issuing a Siri command. It's a little bit annoying but does reduce the risk of someone stealing your smartphone and gaining access to your home.

Regarding the physical installation, it varies between suppliers and following a specific set of instructions. While installing a new lock on your door can be pretty involved for some people because physical work may be required to remove the existing deadbolt and to mount the new one, integration into your HomeKit based smart home is pretty painless. With the Home App open, simply point your iPhone or iPad's camera at the smart lock code, which will get automatically read by the app. Setup is typically confirmed by Home and your smart lock is now ready to be controlled by all of your families iOS devices.

NON-HOMEKIT COMPLIANT SMART HOME PRODUCTS

Although the smart home automation industry is relatively small, it is mature and comes with a mix of established networking protocols. Traditional protocols such as Zigbee, Insteon and Z-Wave are considered to be particularly suitable communication technologies for households.

Apple acknowledged this reality and has responded by providing support within the HomeKit protocol for hardware devices called "bridges" that translate between HomeKit compatible and non-compatible devices. The use of bridges could be quite useful in a number of circumstances. For instance, a tech-savvy household may have gathered a number of smart plugs, light dimmers and security sensors over the years that utilize protocols such as:

- **Z-Wave –** Z-wave is a wireless home control technology that is retrofittable into existing homes. In other words, there is no need to open walls, drill ceilings or rip up carpets. From a technical standpoint, Z-Wave consists of low power radio waves that travel through the walls and floors of your house.

- **Zigbee –** Zigbee is an open public standard for wireless sensor networking that is developed by the Zigbee alliance.

- **Insteon –** Insteon is a company specific protocol that uses both airwaves and high voltage cabling simultaneously to provide communication between smart home devices.

Insight from Gerard:

Currently HomeKit does not fully interoperate with Wi-Fi-based smart home products (Nest, for instance) and has limited support for Bluetooth based devices, which are not HomeKit certified.

Although the homeowner is able to use an iOS app to control these devices, the person is unable to use HomeKit's Siri commands to control these devices. The solution is to purchase a HomeKit hub, which acts as a bridging interface between HomeKit compatible devices the homeowner may purchase over the coming years and the older Z-wave, Insteon and Zigbee equipment that is currently installed.

Now that you have HomeKit connected products up and running in your home, let's talk about how to personalize the HomeKit experience on your phone.

ORGANIZING YOUR SMART HOME DEVICES USING HOMEKIT

HomeKit even has some organizational capabilities. All of our houses consist of a number of different areas that have different requirements in terms of heating, lighting, and sensors. To provide structure within a HomeKit enabled home; the Apple smart home ecosystem allows you to arrange your smart home(s) in a hierarchical manner as follows:

Homes – As the name infers Home is at the very top of the framework used to organize your HomeKit based smart home. It is intended to act as a virtual container for all of your HomeKit enabled connected devices. The Home App comes with default title of 'My Home'. If you are not happy with the default name, then tapping the icon on the top left-hand corner of the home screen within the App allows you to personalize the name of your home.

Rooms – In addition to Home, Rooms are also used to organize your smart home in a structured manner. In the HomeKit system, unique names get applied to each of the rooms in your house. These names are stored in a database on your phone that is accessible via Siri.

Rooms are setup using Apple's own Home App or a third party app that comes with a HomeKit compliant product. Here is how a room setup looks like within Apple's Home App. As you can see; each room will contain a single or indeed multiple HomeKit accessories and scenes.

If for whatever reason; you do not assign a smart device to a room, the Home app will automatically assign to the 'Default Room'.

Insight from Gerard:

It is fair to say that most people will own a single home, however, there are people who own a vacation home or indeed a number of rental properties. For those of you that do have multiple homes, HomeKit provides the capability of configuring multiple properties under one single Apple account. Each home is treated as an entirely separate entity within the Apple smart home ecosystem.

USING SIRI TO CONTROL YOUR HOMEKIT DEVICES

After setting up your HomeKit connected devices, Siri voice commands can be used for control.

With HomeKit all names assigned to homes, rooms and scenes are stored in a common database accessible by Siri. This allows Siri to recognize which part of your smart home to control when voice commands are issued.

The following table describes some popular Siri commands used to control various categories of smart home devices.

Table 2 – Example Siri Commands

HomeKit Product Categories	Popular Siri Commands
Smart Bulbs	• Siri turn on home office light • Siri set the girl's room light to pink (Yes, we have four daughters, so pink is pretty popular in our house J) • Siri set kitchen lights to 50% • Siri turn on the lights
Smart Plugs	• Siri turn kettle on (We like our tea here in Ireland!) • Siri turn on the printer in the office
Smart Locks	• Siri lock the front door • Siri unlock the front door • Siri lock the sliding door • Siri unlock the sliding door
Smart Alarm Sensors	• Siri arm all windows • Siri disarm the alarm
Smart Thermostats	• Siri Set upstairs temperature to 65

Not only can you use Siri to control specific smart home products but you can also give voice commands to your iOS device to run various types of scenes.

Saying 'Hey Siri, Good Morning' will get your household up and running for the day.

To access Siri, all you need to do is press and hold down the microphone button on one of the following devices:

- iPhone
- iPad
- Apple Watch (Press and hold the Digital Crown.)
- Apple TV's Siri remote

While the button is pressed, speak your request.

Once you've finished speaking, simply let go of the button and related instructions will appear on-screen.

After a brief moment, HomeKit and Siri will process your spoken request, initiate the action, and return the results of your voice command on screen.

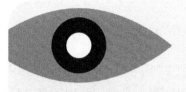

Insight from Gerard:

At the time of writing, there are strong indications that Apple are rumoured to working on a Siri-enabled smart-home speaker to compete with Amazon's echo device and the recently announced Google Home.

USING HOMEKIT ON YOUR WRIST

HomeKit also works on Apple Watches allowing you to communicate with various smart home products. Although our iPhones are awesome, we all tend to drop them in one of our rooms or in the hall once we get home. From an automation perspective, that is a slight issue because in-home presence detection functionality will not operate when at home. In other words, your smart devices will equate the location of your iPhone with your own physical location. So, if you are moving around the house from room to room, your connected bulbs, sensors and thermostats will not be able to pinpoint your movements.

For most people it's perfectly fine, but for those of you who want to increase the "smartness" levels of your property; then consideration should be given to using an Apple Watch configured to use HomeKit.

Apple Watch has three sets of features that are particularly relevant to HomeKit based households, namely: notifications, glances, and queries.

① **HomeKit Watch Notifications** – As the name implies, a notification is a message that appears on your Apple Watch screen. Within the context of a smart home, a notification might pop up when arriving home asking if you want to turn on music and lights in particular rooms. An example of a HomeKit notification alerting you that you accidentally forgot to turn the lights off is shown below.

② **HomeKit Watch Glances** – The second feature that gets used by HomeKit is glances. As the term suggests, glances allow you to take a quick snapshot of things going on in your smart home. Getting an update on temperature levels at your house, for instance, is a popular use of HomeKit glances.

③ **HomeKit Watch Queries** – A recurring ritual each morning for many of us might be questioning ourselves - did I leave the lights on?, did I lock the door on the way out? and so on. With HomeKit, we can now check our wrists to answer basic, but peace of mind effecting questions.

With various sensors built in, Apple Watch has an added advantage in that it can make clear distinctions between the times of the day when you are awake and when you have nodded off to sleep. Feeding this information into your HomeKit based household serves to enhance the "smartness" levels of your home. Refining the behavior of a property to reflect your lifestyle is seen by many in the industry as one of the key benefits of smart home automation systems.

Popular Uses of Apple Watch HomeKit Apps

Various smart home companies have released their own Apple watch friendly apps. Here are some practical uses of combining an Apple Watch with your in-home Homekit devices:

- Quick control of lights and window dressings from your wrist – no need to navigate the interface on your smartphone.

- Receive a notification if you forget to turn one of the lights off when you have left home.

- Receive a prompt when away from home to switch your smart thermostats into "out of town" mode.

- Receive a notification when a security sensor is triggered or you forget to lock the garage door.

- Monitor video feeds from various security cameras.

- Launch some pre-defined smart home automation scenes.

This author believes that the usage list of combining Apple Watches with smart home systems will continue to expand over the coming weeks and years.

CONTROLLING YOUR APPLE HOME OVER THE INTERNET

Inside your home, devices that comply with HomeKit are controllable in a traditional manner (i.e. via an app) and using Siri.

However, to remotely control your HomeKit using voice commands when away from home and use various types of automations, you will need to have a fourth generation Apple TV running tvOS 10 or an iPad running iOS 10 installed on your home network.

The reason for this pre-requisite comes down to security.

Apple wants to ensure that voice commands issued from outside the home are all authenticated prior to telling various HomeKit devices scattered around your home what to do.

Setting up Your Apple TV 4 as a Home Hub

Thankfully, setting up your Apple TV to support remote Siri voice commands and remote control is easy and involves the following three steps:

① **Software Updates** – Make sure that your iPhone, Apple TV or iPad are up to date with the latest iOS version.

② **Update HomeKit Settings** – Here are the key settings that need to be setup on your iOS device:

- On your iPhone or iPad go into the settings section, tap the iCloud option. Scroll down the page and tap the radio button beside the little yellow house icon.

- Next scroll down the page further and make sure that iCloud Keychain is turned to ON mode.

- Next, within the settings menu, you need to scroll down to the HomeKit option.

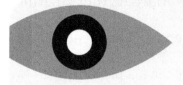

Insight from Gerard:

Make sure that your iOS device and Apple TV are using the same iCloud account.

- Make sure that Home & Mobile Data are both enabled.

③ **Connect Apple TV to your iCloud account–** Once all those settings are set on the iOS device; you will now need to head over to your Apple TV and apply the following settings:

- Navigate to the settings (the gear icon) displayed within the Apple TV interface
- Once in setting, select Accounts
- Then select iCloud
- You will then be prompted for your iCloud username and password. It is likely you already have done this setup previously to make purchases on iTunes and the app store.

Insight from Gerard:

For most people, the setting up of HomeKit on their Apple TVs will simply involve logging out of their iCloud account and back in again.

That's it! The HomeKit functionality will run in the background of your Apple TV. There is no visible indicator of HomeKit functionality on the current iteration of the user interface. The only way that you will know that it is operating correctly is by making a Siri command from a remote location and verifying that the requested action was executed within the walls of your home.

In addition to acting as a hub to facilitate remote access to your smart home products, Apple TV can also be used to extend the wireless range of Bluetooth only smart home gadgets. Let me explain with an example. Some smart locks only support Bluetooth and not Wi-Fi. So if you are upstairs in your bedroom and out of range of the Bluetooth signal, then an instruction ("lock door" for instance), could be sent from your phone over Wi-Fi to the Apple TV and repeated onwards to the lock. In other words, in some instances, the Apple TV can double up as a repeater for extending the signal range of your in-home network.

Setting up Your iPad as a Home Hub

Apple Homekit also supports households that do not own an Apple TV by allowing them instead to use an iPad that remains in the house to provide remote access. Your iPad must be powered and connected to your local Wi-Fi network. Here's how to set it up an iPad as a home hub.

- On your iPad go into the settings section.
- Tap iCloud and sign in with your Apple ID.

- Scroll down and select Home and iCloud keychain and make sure both are turned on.
- Also, go to Settings > Home
- Here you will see a setting called 'Use this iPad as a Home Hub'. Make sure to turn this setting on.

Once you have your hub setup you can start to create different ways of automating your home life.

USING HOMEKIT TO AUTOMATE YOUR HOME

Smart home visionaries dream of a time when the home itself rather than its occupants automatically decide on what systems need to be activated to maximize comfort, safety and security levels. HomeKit brings this vision closer through its support for automation and scenes. A scene defines a set of a set of specific actions that take place for a smart home product or across multiple connected home products all at once. When initially getting your HomeKit network up and running; setting up automation scenes is one of the first things you are going to want to do. HomeKit includes three default scenes:

- **Good Morning -** With this scene, HomeKit devices can be used to automate typical tasks carried out every morning, for instance, opening the shades around the house to let in some natural light and turning the kettle on for your morning tea or coffee.
- **Leave Home -** As the name implies this scene can be setup to lock your door without using a key, switch off key lights around the house and set your smart thermostat to off while you are away.
- **Good Night –** This scene can be setup to do a range of routines such as turning off all lights around the house, reducing down or off your smart thermostat and locking all external doors.

Or, alternatively, you can create your own customized scenes that are specific to your own lifestyle.

There are two ways to activate a scene, namely via an app, Siri or automatically. HomeKit uses software "triggers" to automatically execute scenes without homeowner intervention. HomeKit currently provides support for four different types of triggers, namely:

1. **Location Triggers –** This trigger type uses a technology called geo-location to switch particular connected products on or off when entering or leaving a particular geographical area. For instance, HomeKit allows you to set up a situation where the outside light turns ON as you get closer to the front door.

2. **Time Triggers –** These triggers are linked to time. A common time trigger used in HomeKit enabled homes is the turning on of bedroom lights just before getting out of bed in the mornings. Please also note that sunrise and sunset are also supported within the app.

③ **Connected Device to Connected Device Triggers –** These triggers let use an interaction with a connected device installed in your home to activate automation scenes. For instance, you could trigger the Good Night scene when you turn off your bedroom lamp. This is great because it emulates an activity that you do on a nightly basis.

④ **Sensor Triggers –** As the name infers, HomeKit allows sensors to trigger various flavors of automations. As an example, consider using this to turn on the light when you walk into a dark room. Another popular use of sensor triggers is the activation of emergency scenes once smoke is detected by a HomeKit compliant fire sensor.

HELPING FAMILY MEMBERS INTERACT WITH YOUR SMART HOME

The 'Home' App includes the ability to allow family members or indeed close friends to control your HomeKit enabled home. The ability to share control of your home is done through the 'Home' App and allows you to create individual invites to whoever you feel comfortable with controlling your home.

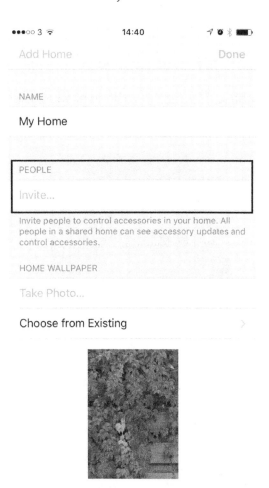

Setting up another family member to control your smart home involves some basic steps, including inviting the other person via their iCloud account, accepting the invite, and starting to use Home or Siri for control purposes only.

Please also note that, people who are classified as share users of your Apple smart home are unable to adjust, remove or add smart home products to the HomeKit system. In other words, access to the system is limited to control only.

SOLVING HOMEKIT ISSUES

Technology is not perfect. Sometimes glitches and problems raise their ugly heads. Instead of getting frustrated, use these easy steps to get your smart home back running. Here are some common problems that can arise.

One of My Connected HomeKit Devices is Not Responding?

If this happens, then check the following:

- First, make sure all of your HomeKit products have a power source; such as the mains or a simple battery.
- Your router is operating correctly if unsure then do a simple reboot.
- On occasions, you may purchase a HomeKit certified product that will have firmware, which requires updating. If you encounter this, then head over to the manufacturer's app and update from there.

Remote Control of My Smart Home Not Working

If you are having trouble controlling various devices, when away from home, then it could be related to issues with your hub. Here are key steps to take to alleviate:

- The power cable for your hub device (i.e. your Apple TV or iPad) is securely connected to a working power source.

- Check that your Apple smart home hub is running the latest version of software.

- Ensure that Home Hub is signed in to iCloud with the correct Apple ID.

If the above steps fail; then try restarting your home hub.

Some of My Automations Are Not Working?

Issues related to automations that use geofencing, are typically related to the following:

- Houses located in remote locations that have weak phone signal will experience unreliability in terms of automation scene activations.

- Location services are not correctly setup on your iPhone, iPad, iWatch or home hub.

FINAL THOUGHTS

Apple Homekit is gaining momentum and is a really exciting time for the home automation industry.

Apple HomeKit allows you to use an iPhone, iPad or indeed an Apple Watch to control a number of smart home products. In essence, your iPhone takes on the role of a smart home automation hub, eliminating some of the complexities associated with these devices.

HomeKit standardizes communication between existing smart home networking technologies, making the management of competing smart home products a smooth and more elegant experience.

This bold initiative by Apple is planning to tackle a big and complex issue, which is how to push smart homes into the mainstream. If the company is successful, then we're going to find ourselves at the beginning of something seriously powerful – enhanced smartness and intelligent levels for millions of properties around the world. In summary, here are a few things you need to understand about the HomeKit ecosystem of products:

- When deployed and setup correctly, HomeKit has various benefits that can enhance your family's safety, security and enjoyment levels.

- With HomeKit, you can use Siri to control various types of connected devices around your home.

- Apple has partnered with core home infrastructure companies such as heating, windows, door locks, security sensors, camera, smart doorbells and garage door manufacturers to incorporate technology required to communicate with the Apple's HomeKit ecosystem.

- HomeKit supports multiple homes. Other properties such as your vacation house or rentals can be configured on your Apple device.

- Not surprisingly, Apple takes HomeKit security and privacy very seriously. Encryption, set-up codes and local storage of information about your home are some of the security and privacy measures used by HomeKit. Manufacturers who want to make their smart home products interoperable with HomeKit add a dedicated wireless chip.

- Cost savings, improved home safety, easy setup and having fun controlling lights on your smartphone are the key benefits of smart bulbs.

- HomeKit smart home sensors allow you to monitor energy usage, detect smoke, measure mold levels, alert you of water leaks and much more.

- Apple uses a dedicated master app called Home to embed smart home functionality directly into the iOS. Your Home App and all of the HomeKit enabled smart home products to work together as a team. Together they make your home come alive in a seamless and simplistic fashion.

- More and more hardware will become available as HomeKit becomes more established.

- You'll need either the newest model of Apple TV or an iPad for remote management features to work, as they act as a hub for accessing your HomeKit devices when you're out of the house.

- Apple is making things far more user-friendly for people to control everything in one place by including smart home control into the Control Centre.

- HomeKit is designed to also work with Apple watches, ideal for receiving update notifications on your wrist of events as they occur in your smart home.

- Adding HomeKit devices to your home is easy and generally, involves taking a picture of a code.

Before we finish, let me temper down my enthusiasm levels by noting that a HomeKit solution leaves out Android users for the moment.

Apple HomeKit is new and evolving and comes with kinks to be ironed out over the coming months and indeed years. The future looks bright for HomeKit and at the time of writing this author believes that Apple is now poised to finally put its full weight behind the smart home!

Thanks for checking out this handbook.

http://homementors.com

@gerardireland

ABOUT THE AUTHOR

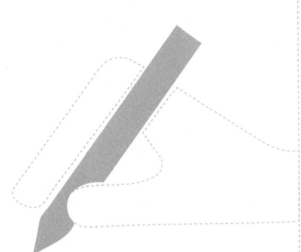

Gerard O'Driscoll is 45 years old and originally from Cork in Ireland, married to Olive with five kids ranging from 5 to 7 years old — so a busy house!

Over the past 20 years, Gerard has served in a variety of management, engineering, and commercial positions in both public and private sectors. Gerard is an accomplished international telecoms expert, educator, serial Internet entrepreneur and angel investor. Other professional achievements include the authoring of various books:

Over the years, Gerard has been given the role as commentator on industry events and trends in the various industry sectors and been quoted in a number of premier business publications. Additionally he has presented papers at a handful of conferences around the world.

In recent years, Gerard has become involved as an angel investor in a portfolio of start-ups & emerging growth companies in mobile apps, e-commerce, e-Learning, subscription commerce, food, Wearables and digital home sectors.

On the education front Gerard hold electronics and information technology qualifications from the University of Limerick in Ireland.

DEDICATION

Apparently behind every important guy is a great girl.☺ This book is dedicated to that girl — my loving wife and girlfriend for over 20++years — Olive!

Of course my dedication extends to our five precious children:

- » Aoife (our little GAA star)☺
- » Ciara (Our little fashion queen)
- » Gerard (AKA Gerdie the hard man)
- » Dearbhla (Our 4 year old little princess)
- » And Baby Aoibhinn (our little Thumbelina, who is now in the terrible two's!).

Also a big dedication goes to my Mother and Father living in Dear Old Skibbereen, West Cork; and my two young brothers — Owen and Brian. And finally my Electronic Production drinking buds!

THE BOOKS COMPANION VIDEO COURSE

To help guide you through building your own Apple Smart Home, I recently produced a companion video training course titled: *How to Build Your Own Smart Home Automation System Using Apple HomeKit Products*.

The regular price of the course is $97, however, for a limited time, you can enroll in the course for $47!

Click Here to get $50 discount off the regular price today before the limited number of coupons run out!

WOULD YOU LIKE TO HEAR MORE ABOUT SMART HOMES & RECEIVE A FREE EBOOK?

We're on the cusp of smart home automation becoming really popular. Nearly everything in your house can be connected. Your garage door, your washer and dryer, your lights, thermostat, door locks, sprinkler system, shades, and more. HomeMentors provide various options in terms of books, courses, and events to increase your knowledge of this space. As a thank you for reading this book, Click Here to Get Your Copy of the '8 Week Blueprint on Building a Smart Home' - A summarized action plan, which you can follow over the coming weeks, months and indeed years.

Oh and if you are half thinking about making money out of installing smart home products then

>> Tap Here and Grab The Free Smart Home Install Toolkit

OTHER BOOKS IN THE ESSENTIAL GUIDE TO SMART HOME AUTOMATION SERIES

Essential Guide to Smart Home Automation Safety & Security

Essential Guide to Smart Bulbs & Lighting Control

Essential Guide to Smart Home Entertainment

Essential Guide to Smart Homes For Aging Adults

Essential Guide to Nest Smart Home Automation System

Essential Guide to Samsung SmartThings Smart Home Automation System

Essential Guide to Apple's HomeKit Smart Home Automation System

Smart Home Automation Essential Guides Box Set

A FAVOR!

Reviews, particularly Amazon are so important when it comes to selling books. I'd like to ask for a small favor. Could you please take a minute or two and leave a review for this book on Amazon? The feedback will not only help sales, but also provides me with encouragement to write books that identify how smart homes can enhance people's lives on a daily basis. Thanks.

A REMINDER ABOUT UPDATES

Before we start, I just want to remind you about the free updates for this book. The Apple HomeKit system is still in its infancy. The product continues to evolve and staying on top of this is my job! So, could I suggest that you **SIGN UP FOR OUR EMAIL LIST** and keep yourself abreast of updates as they happen?

Made in the USA
Las Vegas, NV
13 December 2024